**Election '84 Report #2**

**JCPS**

# Jesse Jackson's Campaign: The Primaries and Caucuses

**Thomas E. Cavanagh**

**Lorn S. Foster**

Election '84 Report #2

# Jesse Jackson's Campaign: The Primaries and Caucuses

Thomas E. Cavanagh

Lorn S. Foster

Joint Center for Political Studies     Washington, D.C.     1984

The Joint Center for Political Studies is a national nonprofit institution that conducts research on public policy issues of special concern to black Americans and promotes informed and effective involvement of blacks in the governmental process. Founded in 1970, the Joint Center provides independent and nonpartisan analyses through research, publication, and outreach programs.

Opinions expressed in Joint Center publications are those of the authors and do not necessarily reflect the views of the other staff, officers, or governors of the Joint Center or of the organizations supporting the center and its research.

We gratefully acknowledge the support of the Rockefeller Foundation and the Ford Foundation, which helped to make this publication possible.

JK
526
1984c

ISBN 0-941410-45-5

Copyright ©1984, Joint Center for Political Studies, Inc.
All Rights Reserved
Printed in the United States of America

1301 Pennsylvania Ave., N.W.
Suite 400
Washington, D.C. 20004

# Contents

| | |
|---|---|
| Foreword | iv |
| The Decision to Run | 1 |
| Campaign Objectives | 2 |
| Black Political Empowerment | 3 |
| A Multiethnic Coalition? | 7 |
| Media Coverage | 11 |
| Campaign Organization and Finance | 12 |
| Implications for the Future | 14 |

Tables

| | | |
|---|---|---|
| 1. | Southern voter registration, 1980-84 | 16 |
| 2. | Turnout changes, 1980-1984, and 1984 first-time voters in Democratic presidential primaries | 17 |
| 3. | Congressional districts in which blacks comprise 20 percent or more of the voting-age population | 18 |
| 4. | 1984 Democratic presidential primary voting by race | 24 |
| 5. | Black 1984 Democratic presidential primary voting by age | 25 |
| 6. | Black voting in Alabama and Georgia primaries | 26 |
| 7. | Jesse Jackson for President Campaign Committee disbursements | 27 |

## Foreword

"Jesse Jackson's Campaign: The Primaries and Caucuses" is the second JCPS Election '84 Report. It provides a preliminary assessment of the Jackson campaign during the Democratic delegate selection process.

As the report points out, Jesse Jackson's objectives were more complex than the usual goal of winning the presidential nomination. Therefore, the authors explore both the purposes of the campaign and the extent to which those purposes were fulfilled. This is not, of course, the last word on the subject, and the Joint Center will publish an in-depth analysis of the campaign and its significance after the November election.

This report was prepared by Thomas E. Cavanagh, research associate, and Lorn S. Foster, senior fellow, under the supervision of Milton D. Morris, director of research at the Joint Center. Much of the data was compiled by Devonda Byers, research assistant. Naima Washington and Panola Golson typed the manuscript, and Constance Toliver formatted the final copy for printing. We are grateful to these and other staff members for their work on this report.

Eddie N. Williams
President
June 1984

Jesse Jackson's presidential campaign marks a political watershed for black America. Jackson has amassed more national convention delegates than any other black man or woman in the nation's history. He has inspired strong and widespread grass-roots enthusiasm in the black community and has raised to prominence a number of issues of special concern to blacks. Although he has had only sporadic success in his vision of a multiethnic "Rainbow Coalition," the concept is likely to play an important role in progressive politics for years to come.

## The Decision to Run

Speculation on a black presidential candidacy grew out of a series of meetings of black political, religious, and civil rights leaders, which the press christened the "Black Leadership Family." The group was organized during the spring of 1983, largely through the initiative of Mayor Richard Hatcher of Gary and Mayor Andrew Young of Atlanta, to assess the status of blacks within the Democratic party. Blacks were dissatisfied with the ineffectual Democratic congressional opposition to President Reagan's initiatives in 1981, as well as the widespread defection of white Democratic party leaders and voters from Chicago mayoral nominee Harold Washington.

In fact, the original impetus for the meetings was to pressure the Democratic National Committee to spur support for Washington's candidacy and to commit resources to a major black voter registration effort. The possibility of a black presidential candidacy was raised as a potential means of obtaining leverage for black interests within the party.

---

Thomas E. Cavanagh is a research associate at the Joint Center. He has taught at Wesleyan University and Trinity College. Most recently he was a guest scholar at the Brookings Institution. A political scientist, he has published widely on congressional behavior and voter turnout.

Lorn S. Foster, a senior fellow at the Joint Center, is on leave from Pomona College in Claremont, California, where he is associate professor of government and black studies. Previously, he was director of the Institute for Ethnic Studies at the University of Nebraska.

In March 1983, the Joint Center published a paper entitled "Outlook for a Black Presidential Candidacy," which served as a background paper for the Black Leadership Family discussions of the topic. The paper identified the possible benefits of a black presidential candidacy as: "giving prominence to issues of special concern to blacks"; "encouraging black voter registration"; "assembling a cohesive black delegate bloc"; and "serving as a trial run for a future black candidacy." The possible costs included: "taking delegates from the more desirable of the viable candidates"; "reducing the eventual nominee's responsiveness to black concerns"; "failing to elect a significant number of black delegates"; "making the Democratic nominee appear the captive of blacks and other 'special interest groups'"; "intensifying racial polarization in the electorate"; and "fragmenting rather than unifying black political leadership." But, the report noted, "a Democratic presidential victory in 1984 is inconceivable without a strong black showing in northern cities and the South. This consideration reduces somewhat the risk of a rift with the Democratic nominee in the event of a black presidential nomination bid," because "whoever wins the Democratic nomination cannot afford to alienate the black vote."

At a meeting in Chicago, on June 20, 1983, the group endorsed the idea of a black presidential candidacy without endorsing a specific individual. Nonetheless, such major black leaders as Detroit Mayor Coleman Young, NAACP President Benjamin Hooks, and National Urban League President John Jacob continued to oppose the idea.

Throughout the spring and summer of 1983, one of the foremost proponents of such a candidacy was Jesse Jackson. Because of his high visibility and popularity among blacks, and his expressions of interest in the possibility of running himself, attention gravitated toward Jackson as a possible candidate. Early polls indicated that such a candidacy held promise: the May 1983 Garth Analysis found him running third in the Democratic nomination race behind Walter Mondale and John Glenn, supported by 9 percent of Democrats nationally and fully 42 percent of black Democrats. He also enjoyed an astounding 78 to 7 percent ratio of "favorable" to "unfavorable" ratings among blacks. Jackson was named "the most important black leader in America" by 51 percent of blacks in an October 1983 ABC News poll, vastly out-distancing Andrew Young (with 8 percent), Martin Luther King, Sr. (4 percent), and Benjamin Hooks (2 percent). No other person was named by more than 1 percent.

### Campaign Objectives

The purpose of a campaign for the presidential nomination is to win a majority of the convention delegates and thereby become a party's candidate. But several factors have made Jesse Jackson's campaign distinctly unusual--particularly his lack of experience as a political officeholder or even political candidate, his controversial career as a civil rights activist, and the roots of his candidacy in a general interest in "a black candidate." Most observers concluded from the outset that his nomination was an unattainable goal, and the election of more than a few hundred delegates was highly improbable. Even the vice-presidential nomination, a traditional consolation prize for unsuccessful presidential candidates, seemed extremely unlikely.

The campaign's objectives, then, and the criteria for evaluating the campaign's success in meeting these objectives are different from those of more traditional presidential campaigns.

The closest modern parallel is the 1968 Democratic campaign of Eugene McCarthy, which had three overriding objectives: to block the renomination of President Lyndon Johnson; to pressure Congress into halting and reversing the escalation of American military involvement in Indochina; and (in the latter stages of the campaign) to expand participation in the delegate selection process beyond the traditional core of party elites. All three of these objectives were in fact achieved. The campaign was therefore a success on its own terms, rather than on the conventional terms of securing the presidential nomination for McCarthy.

The Jackson campaign, like the McCarthy campaign, is in a sense a "symbolic" effort. To some, the fact that it has no hope of culminating in Jackson's nomination means it is futile and pointless. But McCarthy's "symbolic" 1968 nomination campaign had a far more lasting effect on the American political process than did Hubert Humphrey's "victorious" nomination campaign. Jesse Jackson's campaign will probably have an equally lasting effect.

The Jackson campaign appears to have four major objectives. The campaign is achieving success in three of these areas, which together can be considered under the rubric of "black empowerment": to increase black political participation; to alter party rules and state laws to increase the electoral impact of this participation; and to articulate issues and positions of concern to minorities. The fourth objective, the creation of a multiethnic coalition of progressive forces within the Democratic Party, has met with very limited success.

## Black Political Empowerment

### Increasing Black Political Participation

The campaign sought to stimulate black political participation at several levels.

<u>Encouraging black voter registration and turnout.</u> During his "Southern Crusade" of the summer of 1983, Jackson sought to generate widespread political enthusiasm among blacks. His campaign is generally credited with significantly increasing black voter registration, especially in the South. However, much credit is also due to such nonpartisan groups as the A. Philip Randolph Institute, NAACP, Operation Big Vote, Voter Education Project, and PUSH, which conducted voter registration programs that predated the Jackson campaign. These programs were independent of the campaign, although they benefited from the visibility Jackson gave to the goal of black voter participation (Table 1).

NBC found that 20 percent of black primary voters in Florida and Georgia had registered within the previous six months, and CBS found that from 4 to 11 percent of black voters were voting for the first time ever. In most states, black primary turnout increased dramatically over the 1980 level, while white turnout increased far less, or even decreased (Table 2).

<u>Encouraging black candidates to run at lower levels of office.</u> It is too early to judge whether more blacks are running for office because of Jackson's candidacy. Jackson had hoped that his presence on the primary ballot would lend a "coat-tails" advantage to blacks competing concurrently for lower-level nominations. Moreover, the increase in black registration and get-out-the-vote organizing was expected to increase the black turnout in both primary and general election battles. And, in the longer run, the improved turnout was supposed to inspire additional black candidates to run for office by increasing their chances of winning.

Any increase in black candidates could yield important dividends in future years. Black city council members and school board members elected in 1984 could gain the visibility and experience to mount viable campaigns in state legislative, mayoral, and congressional elections in the future.

So far, in 1984, the record is mixed. Black registration gains clearly were a factor in the election of a black candidate, James W. Holley III, as mayor of Portsmouth, VA. However, black Congresswoman Katie Hall of Indiana was defeated in her bid for renomination; black candidates Ken Spaulding and Howard Lee lost congressional bids to unseat incumbent white Democrats in North Carolina; and Roland Burris failed to win the Democratic Senate nomination in Illinois.

<u>Encouraging networking among black political activists.</u> Planning and staffing a presidential campaign requires a veritable army of workers from the national down to the precinct level. The process of identifying and training these people yields an extensive nationwide network of black political operatives possessing a valuable body of expertise, which can be mobilized on behalf of black political interests in the future.

<u>Assembling a cohesive bloc of black convention delegates.</u> At national conventions, delegates tend to take their cues on platform and rules controversies from the candidates whom they are pledged to support. At the 1984 convention for the first time, a large bloc of delegates is pledged to a black candidate.

As of this writing, there are 384 delegates pledged to Jackson, including add-on delegates. Most of them are black. Another 35 delegates pledged to Mayor Harold Washington are considered to be Jackson supporters.

Nor are these the only black delegates to the convention: over 300 of Mondale's delegates are black. Thus, this convention will have both the largest number and the largest proportion of black delegates ever.

## Altering Party Rules and State Laws

The campaign also sought to alter party rules and state laws to accentuate the impact of black participation. Jackson has had major objectives in this area.

<u>Eliminating the runoff primary.</u> In nine Southern states and Oklahoma, a runoff is mandated whenever no candidate receives a majority of the primary vote. The runoff provision is generally believed to harm the chances of black candidates to win nominations wherever blacks are a minority of the electorate, owing to the difficulty black candidates usually have in attracting white support. The issue is a divisive one, both within the Democratic party and among blacks; and some observers feel the issue does not warrant the priority placed upon it by Jackson. Jackson argues, however, that by producing more black candidates, the change would almost certainly lead to the election of more blacks to offices at all levels of government in the South, which is one of his major objectives.

The politics of the issue are quite complex. The major losers would be white Democratic incumbents in areas where a large proportion of the registered Democrats are black. While the chances of black candidates to be nominated in some areas would be increased, the abolition of the run-off election might backfire on black aspirations in such black-majority cities as Atlanta, Birmingham, and Memphis, where a white candidate could conceivably win a single-round primary with a plurality of the vote against two or more black opponents. Furthermore, it is not clear that eliminating run-off primaries would produce more black officeholders as well as more black nominees. If the change succeeded in producing more black nominees, it could benefit Republicans, to the extent that white Democratic voters might defect from black Democratic nominees in general elections.

One compromise position is a runoff requirement when a primary winner fails to receive 40 percent of the vote, as proposed by Governor Richard Riley of South Carolina. This would eliminate situations in which a viable black candidate enjoys a sizable lead in the first round primary, only to lose because of white bloc voting in the runoff. At the same time, it would guard against the nomination of candidates who enjoyed so little support within the party that they would stand virtually no chance in the general election. Jackson has not endorsed the 40 percent compromise, but his delegates supported it overwhelmingly in a resolution passed at the South Carolina state convention in mid-April.

Fully enforcing provisions of the Voting Rights Act. In addition to the runoff primary, Jackson has highlighted several other specific electoral mechanisms he considers violations of the Voting Rights Act. These mechanisms include racial gerrymandering--i.e., diluting the black vote by dispersing it across several districts to minimize the creation of black-majority districts; annexation of white-majority jurisdictions (such as suburbs) to black-majority jurisdictions (such as cities), again in order to dilute the black vote; and the dual registration system in Mississippi, whereby voters must register in one location for state and national elections and another for local elections. Dual registration is a particular hardship for the poor in rural areas, many of whom are black.

The national party has no technical jurisdiction and little practical leverage over such provisions, which must be prevented by the Justice Department under Section 5 of the Voting Rights Act or challenged in court under Section 2. Other than going on record in favor of full enforcement of the Voting Rights Act as it applies to these provisions, there is little the national party can do. The only real sanction available to the national party is to refuse to honor the credentials of national convention delegates from states that have not changed objectionable election laws, and as a practical matter, this is highly unlikely to occur. Even a platform plank by the runoff primary might well be sufficiently controversial to provoke a major platform fight.

Changing delegate selection procedures. Selection of convention delegates, of course, is within the party's own bailiwick. Jackson and others have expressed opposition to provisions they believe hamper the chances of an "outsider" candidate. These include the "threshold," "bonus," and "loophole" provisions. The "threshold" provisions require candidates to receive a minimum share of the vote in a given congressional district (generally about 20 percent) in order to receive any delegates within that district, and a similar share of the statewide vote in order to receive any statewide delegates. Under the "bonus" delegate provision, one congressional district delegate is given to the winner in the district. The "loophole" provision allows the election of delegates district-wide. Because voters are free to vote for all of the delegates on a given candidate's slate in the district, this provision in effect permits winner-take-all voting by congressional district. Furthermore, the large body of delegate seats reserved for state and party elected officials is unlikely to benefit "outsider" candidates as much as well-known centrist candidates with close ties to national party leadership.

The 1984 delegate selection rules were drafted by a special party commission chaired by Governor James Hunt of North Carolina. At the time of the commission's deliberations in 1982, many party leaders and political scientists expressed concern that the party rules were resulting in the nomination of relatively weak candidates such as George McGovern and Jimmy Carter. They felt that such candidates enjoyed little support from the party's leaders or its traditional core constituencies, leaving the party vulnerable to defeat in presidential elections. Thus, the commission attempted to design a nomination process that would reduce the chances of lesser-known candidates to attain the nomination.

At the time, the rules appeared to boost the nomination prospects of Edward Kennedy and Walter Mondale, who were the two most acceptable candidates in the field in the eyes of black leaders. Black criticism of the rules therefore did not begin in earnest until the eve of Jacksons declaration, when the negative implications for a black presidential candidate became fully apparent.

The Hunt Commission rules inhibited the potential of candidates representing any political minority, and not just a racial minority. If Jackson's vote had been more widely and evenly distributed, he could have exceeded the threshold in more districts and won more delegates, although the fact that Jackson's constituency was highly concentrated in a few districts enabled him to clear the threshold in these districts by a wide margin. Reubin Askew, Alan Cranston, and Ernest Hollings also suffered from the Hunt Commission provisions--in some respects more than Jackson, because their constituency bases were less geographically concentrated than Jackson's, making it even more difficult for them to clear the thresholds for district delegates.

Jackson has sometimes seemed to suggest a preference for precise proportionality at all stages of the delegate selection process. He has even attempted to secure additional delegates this year on these grounds in negotiations with party leaders. A strict proportionality would slow the "winnowing" process by which the weaker candidates are eliminated in the early primaries and caucuses. It is rare for any candidate to command a majority in the polls throughout the nomination season, so strictly proportional delegate representation might actually increase the chances for a brokered convention. Ironically, then, the system that would translate popular votes into delegate allocations with the least distortion might result in a "backroom" choice of a nominee free from grass-roots influence.

There are no precedents for reallocating delegates throughout the country by revising the rules after delegates have been selected, as Jackson is currently advocating. (There are precedents for credentials challenges against individual state delegations on the grounds--often spurious--that state delegate selection rules were unfairly enforced or were in violation of national party rules, but that is a different issue.) A few states, such as Alaska, have already relaxed the threshold requirement in response to a memorandum from the Democratic National Committee suggesting that Jackson should receive an equitable share of at-large delegates.

While the 1984 delegate selection procedures are unlikely to be changed to any great extent at this late date, Jackson may have considerable influence in revising the rules to be followed in 1988. Presumably, the party will create another reform commission to deliberate over the rules in 1986. The threshold and loophole provisions are likely to be altered or eliminated.

## Articulating a Progressive Agenda

The third major set of objectives for Jackson's campaign concerns the articulation of an agenda of special concern to minorities. Jackson's presence in the campaign has already given heightened prominence to the issue of South Africa. For example, Mondale made a detailed statement on the issue during the Pittsburgh League of Women Voters' debate in Pittsburgh on April 5, when he called for a cutoff of new American investment if there is no progress on human rights in South Africa. He also advocated a ban on flights into the United States by South African Airways, a ban on International Monetary Fund loans to South Africa, and a ban on the importation of Krugerrands.

One of the more striking aspects of Jackson's campaign has been his emphasis on foreign policy issues. In addition to South Africa, Central America has been a major area of concern. Jackson has stressed opposition to American attempts to destablize Nicaragua and to other forms of military involvement in Central America, and he has sought more open relations with Cuba. He proposed an "even-handed" policy in the Middle East, including recognition of the Palestinian desire for political self-determination; increased trade with the Third World; and a nuclear freeze. His proposals to cut American military spending in absolute terms (rather than merely slow the current rate of spending increase) also have obvious ramifications for deemphasizing American reliance on the military as an instrument of foreign policy.

Jackson's international agenda continues the evolution of a progressive black voice in foreign policy that was evident in Martin Luther King's opposition to the war in Vietnam. By and large, blacks still identify with the liberal side of the "new priorities" debate of the early 1970s, which called for shifting spending away from defense to social programs. Such a position also was reflected in the Congressional Black Caucus budget proposal of 1981, and the recently released "People's Platform" of the National Black Coalition for 1984. Black policy concerns are by no means restricted to the domestic arena, and the increasing black interest in foreign policy is well represented in Jackson's campaign.

On domestic issues, Jackson's positions have been relatively conventional. He has advocated passage of the Equal Rights Amendment, job-training programs, minority set-asides for government contracts, and restoring the social spending cutbacks enacted under the Reagan administration. All of these views are well within the mainstream of Democratic party policy.

A presidential campaign affords an unparalleled opportunity to set forth an agenda for American politics. The issues on which Jackson has focused have been unexpected, particularly his emphasis on foreign policy rather than domestic economic issues. Nonetheless, Jackson is on the verge of success on one subject (South Africa) and may have contributed to keeping party policy from moving substantially to the right to counter the anticipated appeal of Reagan's economic platform to more conservative voters on a number of other issues.

## A Multiethnic Coalition?

Jackson's campaign has been less successful in its effort to forge a multiethnic coalition and win many votes outside the black community. This should not come as a surprise, considering the difficulty that black candidates at lower levels (such as congressional or mayoral races) have encountered in attracting white votes.

The problem was inherent in the use of the campaign as a vehicle for "black empowerment." To the extent that the campaign has concentrated on this objective, it has appeared less relevant to other constituencies. On the other hand, too extensive an emphasis on "non-black" issues might have reduced the symbolic importance of the campaign to blacks and hence its ability to mobilize what everybody considered Jackson's primary political base.

Jackson's announcement speech eloquently struck a balance between these two objectives. He developed the theme of the black experience as a microcosm of the experience of all oppressed peoples in the United States:

> This candidacy is not for blacks only. This is a national campaign growing out of the black experience and seen through the eyes of the black perspective--which is the experience and perspective of the rejected. Because of this experience, I can empathize with the plight of Appalachia because I have known poverty. I know the pain of anti-Semitism because I have felt the humiliation of discrimination. I know firsthand the shame of bread lines and the horror of hopelessness and despair because my life has been dedicated to empowering the world's rejected to become respected. Thus, our perspective encompasses and includes more of the American people and their interest than do most other experiences.

As the campaign got under way, however, strategic realities dictated an initial concentration on mobilizing the black vote. The first rule of campaign targeting is to "go hunting where the ducks are," and Jackson's most promising constituency was clearly black Americans. The congressional districts with heavy black populations indeed proved to be his most potent political base (Table 3).

**Building a Black Base**

Chronologically, his campaign went through three phases in winning black support: an initial phase of hesitation before and immediately after his announcement, during which he and Mondale were essentially tied with about one-third of the black vote apiece; Super Tuesday (March 13), when he edged ahead of Mondale to take a majority of the black vote in Alabama, Florida, and Georgia; and the phase beginning in Illinois on March 20 when he began to win an overwhelming majority (75 percent or more) of the black vote, a share he held in primary states for the remainder of the campaign (Table 4).

Within the black community, Jackson's strongest support came from younger blacks, while older blacks were relatively more likely to vote for Mondale. It was the shift of older blacks from Mondale to Jackson that resulted in the landslide margins he began to roll up in the black community beginning in Illinois (Table 5). No demographic variables other than age systematically distinguish Jackson voters from other black voters (Table 6).

In the South, rural blacks were somewhat more favorable to Jackson than urban blacks. This was especially clear in Alabama, where Mayor Richard Arrington delivered a majority of the black vote to Mondale in Birmingham, while Jackson carried rural blacks by as much as two to one. A similar (though less dramatic) difference appeared in Georgia between blacks in the Atlanta area (where such leaders as Julian Bond and Coretta Scott King supported Mondale) and those in the rest of the state. Although data are lacking, most observers believe Detroit Mayor Coleman Young and the United Auto Workers delivered a majority of the black vote to Mondale in the Michigan caucuses.

In general, where black political leadership lined up organizational strength behind Mondale, Jackson's share of the black vote was held down. In areas where black leaders placed their organizations behind Jackson (as in New Orleans or Washington, D.C.) Jackson's black voter support was extremely high, usually in excess of 80 percent.

To some extent, the likelihood that a major black elected official would endorse Jackson was a function of the black percentage in that official's electoral constituency. Big-city black mayors and black members of congress were most likely to support Jackson if they represent black-majority constituencies (e.g., Mayors Marion Barry of Washington, Kenneth Gibson of Newark, and Richard Hatcher of Gary, and Congressmen John Conyers, Walter Fauntroy, William Gray, Major Owens, Gus Savage, and Louis Stokes) while officials with constituencies at or near a white majority (e.g., Mayors Tom Bradley of Los Angeles, Wilson Goode of Philadelphia, and Andrew Young of Atlanta, and Congressmen Mervyn Dymally, Mickey Leland, and Charles Rangel) were more likely to support Mondale or remain neutral. Politically speaking, it was probably "safer" to heed black grass-roots support for Jackson when an official did not need to worry about adverse reaction from white constituents, politicians, and business leaders. Of course, those blacks who hold office in racially mixed constituencies are likely to have shown responsiveness to white as well as black constituencies in the past and to have ties to the Democratic establishment.

## Appeal to Whites and Hispanics

Jackson has shown very little ability to expand his base beyond the black community. As described in Jackson's announcement speech, the Rainbow Coalition encompasses "whites, blacks, Hispanics, Indian and Native Americans, Asians, women, young people, old people, gay people, laborers, small farmers, small businesspersons, peace activists, and environmentalists." Yet his one-third share of the Hispanic vote in New York was his best showing among any nonblack electorate in any state (Table 4).

Although Jackson's share of the black vote went up as the campaign progressed, his share of the white vote appears to have declined. The extensive literature on black mayoral campaigns has consistently shown three blocs of white voters to be especially receptive to black candidates: young people, the college-educated, and Jews. Jackson's prospects for attracting Jewish support were slim even before the campaign began, because of Jackson's visit to the Palestine Liberation Organization in 1979 and his history of controversial statements with regard to Israel and the Holocaust. They evaporated altogether after he was quoted in the Washington Post referring to Jews as "hymies" and New York City as "Hymietown." His handling of the incident--temporizing before finally admitting to the statements--only compounded the political damage by keeping the issue alive in the press for two full weeks. (By way of contrast, Senator Ernest Hollings referred to Mexican-Americans as "wetbacks" in 1983. He apologized shortly afterward and the issue vanished before it could do lasting damage.)

Aside from Jews, other liberal white constituencies shifted their presidential preferences repeatedly during 1983 and early 1984. A bloc of about 10 to 15 percent of the Democratic electorate appears to have been searching for a progressive alternative to the "centrist" (in Democratic Party terms) Walter Mondale. The very unconventionality of Jackson's candidacy was potentially a major source of appeal to such voters, especially college students. Not being an elected official afforded Jackson freedom to stake out uncompromising positions, because he did not need to fear the reactions of constituents.

A sizable segment of this liberal bloc appears to have supported Cranston because of the nuclear freeze issue in the spring and summer of 1983, supported McGovern after his announcement in August 1983, and then briefly shifted to Jackson in the aftermath of his announcement of his trip to Syria at the turn of the year. Jackson's best showing among whites was probably the 16 percent he received in a Boston Globe poll of the 98 percent white New Hampshire electorate in February. The reporting of the "Hymie" comments in late February undoubtedly contributed to his decline to 5 percent in the actual primary returns.

Another important factor, however, was Glenn's collapse. Glenn's challenge to Mondale had been based on ideology: he claimed that Mondale's issue positions and his constituency base were both too liberal to command support in mainstream America. Glenn highlighted Mondale's vulnerabilities, but he was unable to capitalize on them because he failed to articulate an alternative vision of his own. Moreover, there were not enough conservatives in the Democratic party's primary electorate to dislodge a candidate as squarely positioned in the party's ideological center as Mondale.

Hart, by contrast, challenged Mondale on stylistic grounds, portraying him as a representative of "the past." This could be read by younger liberals as an attack on old-line party bosses and interest group leaders and by older conservatives as an attack on traditional New Deal/Great Society liberalism. Thus, Hart was ideally positioned to capture non-Mondale sentiment on both the left and the right.

The combination of Hart's emergence and the "Hymie" incident evidently foreclosed the possibility that Jackson would attract a significant share of the white liberal vote. By raising doubts about Jackson's adherence to his own professed ideals of tolerance and respect for people of all ethnicities, the ethnic slurs went to the core of Jackson's potential appeal to whites: the perceived sharing of a body of "liberal" values. The controversy over the statements of Minister Louis Farrakhan, and Jackson's long refusal to repudiate his support, only aggravated the doubts of white liberals on this score.

The net effect was to set a very low ceiling on Jackson's share of the white vote. He failed to receive more than 9 percent of the white vote in any state for which exit poll results are available, despite his impressive showings in some of the later debates. A Louis Harris poll found that a plurality of those who watched the Columbia University debate with Hart and Mondale (moderated by Dan Rather) felt that Jackson had "won" the debate; yet he received only 6 percent of the white vote in New York.

Jackson's problems with Hispanics are of a somewhat different nature. Because Hispanics perceived Jackson's campaign as being heavily black-oriented, they apparently felt like junior partners in the Rainbow Coalition. Most major Hispanic leaders endorsed Mondale.

Jackson's 34 percent share of the Hispanic vote (largely Puerto Rican) in New York was mainly a result of local factors. Blacks and Puerto Ricans have a long history of working together politically in New York, backing one another's candidates and lobbying together in the state legislature. Minority hostility toward Mayor Ed Koch is currently encouraging speculation about a black mayoral candidate to oppose his reelection bid in 1985. Thus, the New York presidential primary may have been a "warm up" for the mayoral race in the same sense that the high black turnout in the Illinois governor's race in 1982 proved to be a harbinger of the black activism that unseated Chicago Mayor Jane Byrne and elected Harold Washington in 1983.

During the campaign, Jackson downplayed the appeal to traditional social values that was a staple of his speeches before black audiences for many years. In such appearances, he had often emphasized self-reliance, discipline, education, the family, the church, and black entrepreneurial activity. This message is not often associated with liberal social and economic policies, and it is one that white America generally does not associate with blacks. Jackson might well have improved his standing among whites generally and Hispanics in particular by discussing these values more frequently in his campaign. On occasions when he did, the response was favorable.

For example, in the Columbia University debate, when Dan Rather asked each candidate for an example of a sacrifice he would ask of the American people, Jackson talked eloquently of the need for parents to ensure that their children did not slight their homework to watch television. With that response, Jackson spoke not as a "black candidate" but as a concerned parent. By more fully incorporating this broadly appealing side of his persona into his campaign message, Jackson might have fostered a constructive public dialogue between the races.

Reintegrating the concerns of American liberalism with more traditional social values has been a successful theme for others, most notably New York Governor Mario Cuomo. For Jackson, it could have paid dividends in the form of goodwill and a sympathetic white hearing for black political aspirations. The benefits to the liberal cause in general could have been even greater.

Mel King, a former black state senator, caused a flurry of excitement by qualifying for the run-off in his 1983 mayoral campaign in Boston, although he lost the run-off to Raymond Flynn. King was highly innovative in crafting issue appeals to explore such possibilities of interracial dialogue. He made the concept of the Rainbow Coalition an organizing principle for his campaign by framing issues in such a way as to scramble existing racial divisions and rearrange political blocs along class lines. For example, he advocated a shift from at-large to district representation in the Boston city council, which furthered the aspirations of the South Boston Irish as well as blacks. He also proposed that half of all construction jobs on city contracts be reserved for city residents--in effect creating "affirmative action for white people," and recasting the whole affirmative action debate as a positive-sum game for Boston residents rather than a negative-sum game between the races. Framing issues and policies with this kind of creativity can do a great deal to enhance the opportunities for coalition building.

## Media Coverage

The Jackson campaign has been a difficult story for the media to cover. On the one hand, the media have been reluctant to appear overly critical of Jackson for fear of appearing racist. On the other hand, they fear appearing unprofessional by withholding criticism and giving Jackson a "free ride." One result has been a tendency toward fairly literal reporting of Jackson's speeches and the enthusiastic response they often receive, in contrast to the "inner political motive" variety of speculation that has characterized reporting on the other candidates. Coverage of Jackson has in this respect been rather less subjective than the coverage of Hart or Mondale.

The "symbolic" nature of the campaign has proven to be a major source of difficulty to the media. While it is undoubtedly true that Jackson's chances of nomination were virtually nil, the frequent repetition of this assertion (no matter how accurate) risked taking on the quality of a self-fulfilling prophecy. The ordinary criteria of electing delegates and winning primaries were largely irrelevant to the true meaning of Jackson's effort. The media were therefore shorn of their normal methods of evaluating the success of a presidential campaign.

The constant references to Jackson as a "black presidential candidate" may have reinforced an impression among whites that Jackson was a candidate only for blacks. This theme has become more prominent in recent weeks, with the propagation of the statement that Jackson "is really running to be president of black America" (whatever that means). For example, Marvin Kalb asked on "Meet the Press," "Are you a black man who happens to be an American running for the presidency, or are you an American who happens to be a black man running for the presidency?" As Jackson noted in reply, "You ask a funny Catch-22 kind of question." The dichotomy between blackness and Americanism implicit in the question can be interpreted as a casual slur on Jackson's patriotism, if not the patriotism of black America in general.

The result of such dilemmas has been a curiously one-dimensional quality to much of the media coverage, especially in the early phases of the campaign. Jackson has been "good copy." His dynamic presence in public appearances was sufficient to attract heavy television news coverage. Jackson's "free media" exposure reached a peak around the time of the expedition to Syria. Following the "Hymie" incident and the national media coverage of Louis Farrakhan's remarks on Washington Post reporter Milton Coleman, who had reported Jackson's use of the term "hymie," the tone of the media coverage and commentary took a sharply negative turn. The media seemed almost relieved to be able to criticize a black candidate in the name of defending liberal values.

## Campaign Organization and Finance

From its inception, Jesse Jackson's presidential effort has been organized more like a movement than an election campaign. Its structure derives more from the black church and the civil rights movement than from traditional electoral politics. Grass-roots activity in many local areas preceded any direction from the national campaign headquarters.

The result was considerable confusion and lack of coordination. In the days immediately following Jackson's announcement of his candidacy, there weren't even enough telephone lines in the Washington national headquarters for operatives desiring to establish local offices to make contact with the national campaign. Since the announcement came on November 3, much later than that of any of the other candidates, there was little time to gather signatures or file papers to get on state ballots. Indeed, the campaign came within a few hours of missing the filing deadline in the critical early New Hampshire primary.

The late start also hampered fund-raising activity. In contrast to the draft-Kennedy movement in 1979, which had raised money through direct mail for an exploratory committee effort well before Kennedy's formal entry, Jackson had done no serious fund-raising prior to his announcement. To qualify for federal matching funds, a presidential candidate must receive at least $5,000 in each of 20 states, with no more than $250 coming from any one individual. The papers requesting matching funds were not filed with the Federal Election Commission until January 13, 1984.

Cash flow was a major problem. Had an exploratory draft-Jackson committee tested a direct-mail list prior to his announcement, a proven list could have been tapped to raise the money necessary to qualify for matching funds immediately after his announcement, and the funds could have been received by January 1, 1984. Such a list also might have yielded an impressive list of grass-roots organizers and fund-raisers.

The black population generally is a difficult one from which to raise campaign funds. The Jackson campaign targeted congressional districts that are 20 percent or more black (the same target list as for voters) as its chief fund-raising areas. As can be seen from Table 3, the median black income level in most of these districts is quite low. The lack of disposable income among such families limits the potential for fund-raising, although a few areas (such as suburban Los Angeles, South Side Chicago, Gary, Queens, Detroit, and Washington and its suburbs) stand out as having significant potential nonetheless. As of April 30, Jackson had raised $ 3.4 million, according to the Federal Election Commission (Table 7).

The black church was an important element in the Jackson campaign. Blacks ministers frequently emerged as the chairmen of local Jackson organizations. Virtually everywhere, black ministers solicited both financial and organizational support from their congregations, often through the simple expedient of "passing the plate" during a service. The national Jackson for President Campaign Committee even sent a memorandum to thousands of black ministers in March detailing how they could raise funds for the candidate without violating federal election law. The first Sunday in April was set aside as "A Jackson for Jackson Day," a plea for individual $20 contributions in black churches across the nation.

Television debate parties, concerts, and rallies also were used to raise a money for the campaign. Jackson himself frequently ended his campaign appearances with a personal appeal for contributions. It is important to note that cash contributions are not eligible to be matched with federal funds; to qualify for matching, a contribution must be in the form of a check or money order accompanied by the contributor's name and address. Thus, his disproportionate reliance on cash placed Jackson at a disadvantage compared to the other candidates.

Jackson's pattern of campaign spending was also quite unusual. Travel was the campaign's largest reported expenditure item. The second largest was a sizable amount of money set aside for state committees. The use of these funds has not been adequately documented, and the Federal Election Commission has charged that this is a violation of federal election law. Advertising is ordinarily the largest single expenditure in a presidential campaign: it is not uncommon for half of the total budget to be used for television ads alone. Yet the Jackson campaign had earmarked less than $10,000 for advertising through the end of February. No money whatever was spent on television until the June 5 California primary, and very little was spent on radio. Nor did the campaign spend any money on fund-raising until January 1984.

The lack of a paid media campaign left Jackson at the mercy of the news coverage in the "free media" to get his message across. While he has been successful at generating visibility and coverage, he has had no control over the <u>content</u> of this coverage, which restrained his ability to craft a public image through the use of broadcast advertising.

The disarray of the campaign was fully manifest in the scheduling operation. The candidate's calendar of appearances often changed from day to day or even hour to hour on the whim of the candidate, and the press corps frequently had inadequate time to file stories or even make travel arrangements. The difficulties of life aboard the "Rainbow Express" (the campaign plane) were occasionally reflected in a grumpy tone of coverage, but more importantly, they detracted from the campaign's ability to generate full coverage, which is especially important to a campaign that is underfinanced and therefore highly dependent on "free media."

Another problem was that the campaign scheduling was not always in line with the strategic priorities of the campaign. For example, during the week before Super

Tuesday, one might have expected the campaign to be devoting all its time to Alabama, Florida, and Georgia. Yet the candidate also undertook appearances in Massachusetts, Michigan, Illinois, Arkansas, and Kentucky, which diverted precious resources of time and travel money. This curious scheduling may have been partially responsible for Jackson's lower showing among blacks on Super Tuesday than during later stages of the campaign.

### Implications for the Future

Several recent analyses of the Jackson campaign (including cover stories in Time and The New Republic) have concentrated on its potential for divisiveness. Two groups in particular have shown some signs of a reaction against the Jackson campaign: Jews and southern whites. Jewish concerns about Jackson's sympathy for the Palestinian cause have been exacerbated by comments from Jackson that many Jews consider anti-Semitic. Although blacks and Jews have been allies in the civil rights movement for years, some basic conflicts of interest and perception on specific issues such as quotas have led to tensions in black-Jewish political relations over the past few years.

In the South, Jackson has received only a tiny share of white votes. While black turnout has been increasing in most of the Southern primaries, white turnout has been much less impressive. In Louisiana, Governor Edwin Edwards's call for a boycott of the presidential primary clearly held down white turnout. In the rest of the South, the mediocre white turnout may reflect a lack of interest in any of the three major Democratic contenders; or perhaps many Southern white Democrats have already decided to vote for Reagan. More ominously for blacks, it may signal disenchantment with the more visible role of blacks in both state and national Democratic party politics, and a resultant drift to the Republicans. But Republican benefits from racial backlash are likely to be tempered by the party's "country club" image. Many blue-collar southern whites turned out to vote for "populist" Democratic candidates in the 1982 midterm elections, especially in states like Alabama and the Carolinas, where layoffs in the steel, furniture, and textile industries heightened class distinctions between the two parties.

One state where race has become a more or less explicit issue is North Carolina. Senator Jesse Helms' opposition to the Martin Luther King holiday bill has become a major line of attack against Democratic opponent James Hunt. Controversies over Gary Mayor Richard Hatcher and the current turbulence of Chicago politics contributed to black Congresswoman Katie Hall's loss in her renomination bid in Indiana's 1st congressional district. It remains to be seen whether a pattern of white racial appeals will appear in campaigns at the state and local level in response to Jackson's campaign and the publicity over increasing black participation.

Such controversies should not obscure the very real accomplishments of the Jackson campaign. It has succeeded in many of its major objectives. Black registration and turnout are increasing; a largely black Jackson delegate contingent of nearly 400 was elected; networks of black activists were formed at the local level; and breakthroughs have already been achieved in raising such issues as South Africa and the runoff primary to a higher level of significance. The Jackson campaign has proven to be an efficacious vehicle to hasten the process of black political empowerment.

Above all, both black and white Americans have become accustomed to the concept and the reality of a black candidate competing for the presidency in a serious nationwide campaign. Thus, the Jackson candidacy has provided a source of inspiration that may someday carry a black into the White House. Long after the controversies of this year are forgotten, the legacy of Jesse Jackson as a political pioneer will live on.

**Tables**

Table 1. Southern voter registration, 1980-84.

|  | White Registration |  |  | Black Registration |  |  |
|---|---|---|---|---|---|---|
| State | 1980 | 1984 | Change | 1980 | 1984 | Change |
| Alabama | 1,700,000 | 1,664,000 | -36,000 | 350,000 | 482,000 | +132,000 |
| Arkansas | 1,056,000 | 964,000 | -92,000 | 130,000 | 155,000 | +25,000 |
| Florida | 4,331,000 | 4,337,000 | +6,000 | 489,000 | 517,000 | +28,000 |
| Georgia | 1,800,000 | 1,787,000 | -13,000 | 450,000 | 512,000 | +62,000 |
| Louisiana | 1,550,000 | 1,609,000 | +59,000 | 465,000 | 535,000 | +70,000 |
| Mississippi | 1,152,000 | 1,144,000 | -8,000 | 330,000 | 406,000 | +76,000 |
| No. Carolina | 2,314,000 | 2,369,000 | +55,000 | 440,000 | 565,000 | +125,000 |
| So. Carolina | 916,000 | 848,000 | -68,000 | 320,000 | 331,000 | +11,000 |
| Tennessee | 2,200,000 | 2,082,000 | -118,000 | 300,000 | 348,000 | +48,000 |
| Texas | 6,020,000 | 6,042,000 | +22,000 | 620,000 | 720,000 | +100,000 |
| Virginia | 1,942,000 | 1,908,000 | -34,000 | 360,000 | 378,000 | +18,000 |
| Total | 24,981,000 | 24,754,000 | -227,000 | 4,254,000 | 4,949,000 | +695,000 |

Source: Data from *American Political Report*, May 18, 1984. Some data from the Voter Education Project.

Table 2. Turnout changes, 1980-1984, and 1984 first-time voters in Democratic presidential primaries.

| State | Turnout change, 1980-84 Black areas | Turnout change, 1980-84 State total | First-time voters Black | First-time voters White | First-time voters Total |
|---|---|---|---|---|---|
| Alabama | +87% | +71% | n.a. | n.a. | n.a. |
| Florida | +38 | + 7 | n.a. | n.a. | n.a. |
| Georgia | +14 | -34 | n.a. | n.a. | n.a. |
| Illinois | +19 | +37 | n.a. | n.a. | n.a. |
| New York | +127 | +37 | 9% | 1% | 4% |
| Pennsylvania | +32 | - 2 | 5 | 3 | 3 |
| Tennessee | +58 | + 7 | 4 | 4 | 4 |
| Indiana | +29 | +17 | 4 | 5 | 5 |
| Maryland | +33 | + 1 | 11 | 4 | 6 |
| North Carolina | +53 | +18 | 11 | 6 | 8 |
| Ohio | +36 | +21 | 5 | 4 | 4 |
| New Jersey | +82 | +19 | 7 | 2 | 3 |
| California | n.a. | n.a. | 11 | 3 | 5 |

Source: CBS News.

Note: "Black areas" are precincts in which blacks comprise 80 percent or more of the population. "First-time voters" refers to percentage of the CBS/New York Times exit poll respondents who said they were voting for the first time in the presidential primaries.

n.a. not available.

Table 3. Congressional districts in which blacks comprise 20 percent or more of the voting-age population.

| State/District | Location | Black voting-age percentage | Hispanic voting-age percentage | District-level Delegates | District-level Alternates | Black median family income in 1979 (dollars) |
|---|---|---|---|---|---|---|
| **Alabama** | | | | | | |
| 1 | Mobile | 27.7 | 1.0 | 5 | 2 | 9,879 |
| 2 | Montgomery | 27.4 | 1.0 | 5 | 2 | 9,424 |
| 3 | Anniston | 25.2 | 0.9 | 5 | 2 | 10,006 |
| 6 | Birmingham | 31.5 | 0.6 | 5 | 2 | 11,468 |
| 7 | Tuscaloosa | 29.7 | 0.9 | 5 | 2 | 8,803 |
| **Arkansas** | | | | | | |
| 4 | Pine Bluff | 24.6 | 0.7 | 7 | 2 | 8,832 |
| **California** | | | | | | |
| 8 | Oakland-Berkeley | 24.1 | 5.7 | 6 | 2 | 12,759 |
| 28 | Los Angeles-Inglewood | 41.9 | 26.0 | 8 | 2 | 15,448 |
| 29 | Los Angeles-Downey | 45.7 | 28.2 | 8 | 2 | 10,580 |
| 31 | Compton-Carson | 31.0 | 21.7 | 7 | 2 | 17,145 |
| **District of Columbia**[a] | | | | | | |
| 1 | Wards 1,2,6,8 | 65.3 | 3.6 | 5 | 1 | n.a. |
| 2 | Wards 3,4,5,7 | 66.2 | 2.0 | 6 | 2 | n.a. |

| | | | | | |
|---|---|---|---|---|---|
| Florida | | | | | |
| 2 | Tallahassee | 21.9 | 1.2 | 5 | 9,015 |
| 3 | Jacksonville | 24.6 | 1.7 | 5 | 10,513 |
| 17 | Miami (North) | 21.9 | 24.2 | 5 | 14,217 |
| Georgia | | | | | |
| 1 | Savannah | 30.1 | 1.1 | 4 | 9,523 |
| 2 | Albany | 32.3 | 0.9 | 5 | 9,171 |
| 3 | Columbus | 31.4 | 1.5 | 5 | 10,307 |
| 5 | Atlanta | 60.1 | 1.1 | 5 | 11,658 |
| 8 | Macon | 31.7 | 0.8 | 6 | 10,225 |
| 10 | Augusta | 22.9 | 1.3 | 4 | 10,741 |
| Illinois | | | | | |
| 1 | Chicago (South Side) | 90.2 | 1.0 | 9 | 13,194 |
| 2 | Chicago (Lake Calumet) | 66.4 | 6.6 | 8 | 17,772 |
| 7 | Chicago (West Side) | 59.8 | 4.4 | 7 | 11,258 |
| Indiana | | | | | |
| 1 | Gary | 21.9 | 7.0 | 6 | 17,816 |
| 10 | Indianapolis | 24.8 | 0.9 | 6 | 14,679 |

Table 3 (Continued)

| State/District | Location | Black voting-age percentage | Hispanic voting-age percentage | District-level Delegates | District-level Alternates | Black median family income in 1979 (dollars) |
|---|---|---|---|---|---|---|
| Louisiana | | | | | | |
| 2 | New Orleans | n.a | n.a | 4 | 1 | n.a |
| 4 | Shreveport | 28.7 | 1.9 | 5 | 1 | 10,265 |
| 5 | Monroe | 27.9 | 0.9 | 5 | 1 | 7,715 |
| 6 | Baton Rouge | 22.6 | 1.5 | 5 | 2 | 10,972 |
| 8 | Alexandria | 35.7 | 1.5 | 5 | 2 | 9,805 |
| Maryland | | | | | | |
| 5 | Prince George's County | 31.3 | 2.2 | 5 | 2 | 22,614 |
| 7 | Baltimore (West) | 69.6 | 0.8 | 6 | 2 | 13,094 |
| Michigan | | | | | | |
| 1 | Detroit-Highland Park | 66.1 | 1.8 | 8 | 3 | 18,317 |
| 13 | Detroit (Central) | 67.5 | 2.7 | 7 | 2 | 10,841 |

| | | | | | |
|---|---|---|---|---|---|
| Mississippi | | | | | |
| 1 | Tupelo | 22.6 | 0.7 | 5 | 9,532 |
| 2 | Mississippi Delta | 54.0 | 1.0 | 5 | 7,447 |
| 3 | Meridian | 27.5 | 0.8 | 5 | 9,121 |
| 4 | Jackson | 40.6 | 0.8 | 5 | 9,861 |
| Missouri | | | | | |
| 1 | St. Louis (North) | 46.1 | 0.8 | 6 | 13,316 |
| 5 | Kansas City | 19.8 | 2.4 | 6 | 14,671 |
| New Jersey[b] | | | | | |
| New York | | | | | |
| 6 | Queens (Jamaica) | 46.7 | 8.3 | 6 | 18,378 |
| 11 | Brooklyn (Bedford-Stuyvesant) | 46.6 | 34.1 | 5 | 9,730 |
| 12 | Brooklyn (Crown Heights) | 78.2 | 9.4 | 5 | 12,218 |
| 16 | Manhattan (Harlem) | 49.2 | 34.7 | 6 | 10,225 |
| 18 | Bronx (South) | 44.4 | 48.5 | 5 | 9,012 |

21

Table 3 (Continued)

| State/District | Location | Black voting-age percentage | Hispanic voting-age percentage | District-level Delegates | District-level Alternates | Black median family income in 1979 (dollars) |
|---|---|---|---|---|---|---|
| North Carolina | | | | | | |
| 1 | Cape Hatteras | 31.9 | 0.9 | 5 | 2 | 10,000 |
| 2 | Durham | 36.5 | 0.8 | 5 | 2 | 10,768 |
| 3 | Goldsboro | 25.2 | 1.5 | 4 | 1 | 10,017 |
| 7 | Fayetteville | 25.4 | 2.2 | 4 | 1 | 10,088 |
| 9 | Charlotte | 20.8 | 0.8 | 5 | 2 | 12,543 |
| Ohio | | | | | | |
| 21 | Cleveland (East) | 58.2 | 0.9 | 7 | 2 | 14,822 |
| Pennsylvania | | | | | | |
| 1 | Philadelphia (South) | 28.8 | 7.4 | 9 | 3 | 9,435 |
| 2 | Philadelphia (West) | 75.7 | 1.1 | 9 | 3 | 12,399 |
| South Carolina | | | | | | |
| 1 | Charleston | 29.4 | 1.6 | 4 | 1 | 10,508 |
| 2 | Columbia | 31.9 | 1.2 | 5 | 2 | 11,384 |
| 3 | Anderson | 20.1 | 0.7 | 5 | 1 | 11,777 |
| 5 | Rock Hill | 29.4 | 0.8 | 5 | 2 | 11,430 |
| 6 | Florence | 36.7 | 1.0 | 5 | 2 | 10,248 |

| | | | | | |
|---|---|---|---|---|---|
| Tennessee | | | | | |
| 5 | Nashville | 19.8 | 0.7 | 6 | 2 | 12,712 |
| 9 | Memphis | 50.6 | 0.7 | 7 | 2 | 10,322 |
| Texas[c] | | | | | |
| 13 | Harris County | 48.6 | 9.7 | 5 | 2 | n.a. |
| 15 | Harris County | 23.6 | 30.1 | 4 | 1 | n.a. |
| 23 | Dallas County | 46.6 | 13.3 | 4 | 1 | n.a. |
| Virginia | | | | | |
| 1 | Newport News | 29.2 | 1.2 | 5 | 2 | 12,433 |
| 2 | Norfolk | 21.0 | 2.0 | 4 | 1 | 11,035 |
| 3 | Richmond | 26.5 | 0.8 | 5 | 2 | 14,335 |
| 4 | Portsmouth | 37.3 | 1.0 | 5 | 2 | 12,507 |
| 5 | Danville | 22.4 | 0.7 | 5 | 1 | 12,165 |
| Wisconsin | | | | | |
| 5 | Milwaukee (North Side) | 22.3 | 1.7 | 7 | 2 | 12,551 |

Source: Data from U.S. Bureau of the Census, Congressional Data Profiles: 98th Congress (Washington: Government Printing Office, 1983).

n.a. - not available

[a] The District of Columbia has two "delegate districts," although it has no congressional districts.

[b] In New Jersey, delegates are allocated by specially designated "delegate districts," for which data were not available at press time.

[c] In Texas, delegates are allocated by state senatorial districts.

Table 4. 1984 Democratic presidential primary voting by race.

|  |  | Black percentage of sample | Blacks |  |  |  | White percentage of sample | Whites |  |  |  |
|---|---|---|---|---|---|---|---|---|---|---|---|
| State | Date | | Glenn | Hart | Jackson | Mondale | | Glenn | Hart | Jackson | Mondale |
| Alabama | 3/13 | 40% | 1% | 1% | 50% | 47% | 56% | 32% | 37% | 1% | 29% |
| Georgia | 3/13 | 28 | 1 | 5 | 61 | 30 | 69 | 25 | 38 | 1 | 32 |
| Illinois | 3/20 | 25 | — | 4 | 79 | 17 | 69 | — | 45 | 4 | 47 |
| New York | 4/3 | 23 | — | 3 | 87 | 8 | 70 | — | 36 | 6 | 57 |
| Pennsylvania | 4/10 | 16 | — | 3 | 77 | 18 | 82 | — | 43 | 4 | 50 |
| Tennessee | 5/1 | 26 | — | 2 | 76 | 22 | 71 | — | 43 | 2 | 51 |
| Texas* | 5/5 | 33 | — | 1 | 83 | 16 | 56 | — | 37 | 4 | 50 |
| Indiana | 5/8 | 14 | — | 9 | 71 | 20 | 85 | — | 51 | 3 | 44 |
| Maryland | 5/8 | 24 | — | 2 | 83 | 13 | 73 | — | 35 | 5 | 53 |
| No. Carolina | 5/8 | 27 | — | 1 | 84 | 13 | 69 | — | 41 | 3 | 46 |
| Ohio | 5/8 | 19 | — | 3 | 81 | 15 | 79 | — | 50 | 5 | 44 |
| California | 6/5 | | — | 5 | 78 | 16 | | — | 48 | 9 | 40 |
| New Jersey | 6/5 | | — | 2 | 86 | 11 | | — | 38 | 4 | 56 |

Source: CBS/New York Times exit surveys.

*Sample of caucus participants

Table 5. Black 1984 Democratic presidential primary voting by age.

| State | Date | Blacks under age 50 | Blacks age 50 and over |
|---|---|---|---|
| Alabama | 3/13 | | |
| Hart | | 4% | 3% |
| Jackson | | 67 | 45 |
| Mondale | | 26 | 51 |
| Florida | 3/13 | | |
| Hart | | 7 | 4 |
| Jackson | | 67 | 51 |
| Mondale | | 26 | 43 |
| Georgia | 3/13 | | |
| Hart | | 4 | 5 |
| Jackson | | 74 | 68 |
| Mondale | | 21 | 26 |
| Illinois | 3/20 | | |
| Hart | | 9 | 7 |
| Jackson | | 74 | 76 |
| Mondale | | 15 | 16 |
| New York | 4/3 | | |
| Hart | | 2 | 2 |
| Jackson | | 93 | 81 |
| Mondale | | 5 | 17 |
| Pennsylvania | 4/10 | | |
| Hart | | 7 | 12 |
| Jackson | | 77 | 65 |
| Mondale | | 16 | 23 |

Source: NBC News exit surveys.

Table 6. Black voting in Alabama and Georgia primaries.

|  | Alabama |  | Georgia |  |
|---|---|---|---|---|
|  | Jackson | Mondale | Jackson | Mondale |
| TOTAL SAMPLE | 50% | 47% | 61% | 30% |
| **Age** | | | | |
| 18-29 years old | 59 | 36 | 64 | 31 |
| 30-44 | 68 | 30 | 64 | 25 |
| 45-59 | 41 | 55 | 65 | 33 |
| 60 and older | 34 | 64 | 58 | 32 |
| **Sex** | | | | |
| Men | 52 | 43 | 58 | 30 |
| Women | 50 | 49 | 64 | 30 |
| **Family income** | | | | |
| under $12,500 | 53 | 46 | 63 | 33 |
| $12,500 to $25,000 | 37 | 60 | 65 | 26 |
| Over $25,000 | 64 | 31 | 58 | 30 |
| **Political leaning** | | | | |
| Liberal | 55 | 43 | 69 | 27 |
| Moderate | 46 | 52 | 57 | 32 |
| Conservative | 55 | 41 | 63 | 30 |

Source: CBS/New York Times exit survey data published in the New York Times, March 15, 19

Table 7. Jesse Jackson for President Campaign Committee disbursements, October 1, 1983-April 30, 1984.

| Disbursements | October-December | January | February | March | April | Total |
|---|---|---|---|---|---|---|
| Telephone | $28,591.28 | $15,776.13 | $20,098.76 | $87,771.46 | $62,747.95 | $214,985.58 |
| Payroll | 46,245.15 | 39,720.23 | 41,598.92 | 37,603.44 | 66,949.72 | 232,117.46 |
| Travel | 55,887.93 | 129,618.33 | 171,194.50 | 235,752.60 | 277,136.51 | 869,589.87 |
| Contracted services | 23,621.83 | 36,938.65 | 49,207.48 | 76,505.79 | 108,308.15 | 294,581.90 |
| Political events | -0- | 7,815.22 | 7,858.91 | 1,020.16 | 3,111.22 | 19,805.51 |
| Media | -0- | 327.00 | 6,060.96 | 40,912.96 | 111,900.80 | 159,201.72 |
| Fundraising | -0- | 4,903.00 | 7,092.32 | 16,531.58 | 334,520.00 | 363,046.90 |
| Committee transfers | -0- | -0- | 309,691.88 | 356,012.05 | 159,180.95 | 824,884.88 |
| Administrative | 13,608.98 | 48,773.59 | 27,450.45 | 39,642.82 | 31,463.10 | 160,938.94 |
| Office rental | 11,423.29 | 98,603.60 | 19,157.89 | 5,077.99 | 3,442.60 | 137,705.37 |
| Miscellaneous | 3,706.67 | 43,371.48 | 55,255.27 | 10,317.73 | 9,183.75 | 121,834.90 |
| Total | $183,085.13 | $425,847.23 | $714,667.34 | $907,148.58 | $1,167,944.75 | $3,398,693.03 |

Source: Data from Federal Election Commission.

## SELECTED JCPS PUBLICATIONS

*Black Americans and the Shaping of U.S. Foreign Policy: Proceedings of a JCPS Roundtable,* 1981. ISBN 0-941410-18-8. $4.95

*Black Elected Officials and their Constituencies,* Thomas E. Cavanagh and Denise Stockton, 1983. ISBN 0-941410-28-5. $4.95.

*Black Employment in City Government, 1973-1980,* Peter Eisinger, 1983. ISBN 0-941410-32-3. $4.95.

*Black Politics 1980,* JCPS Office of Research, 1980. ISBN 0-941410-10-2.
  --*A Guide to the Democratic National Convention.* ISBN 0-941410-11-0. $4.95.
  --*A Guide to the Republican National Convention.* ISBN 0-941410-12-9. $4.95.

*Blacks on the Move: A Decade of Demographic Change,* William P. O'Hare, Jane-yu Li, Roy Chatterjee, and Margaret Shukur, abridged by Phillip Sawicki, 1982. ISBN 0-941410-25-0. $4.95.

*The Changing Patterns of Black Family Income, 1960-1982,* Henry E. Felder, 1984. ISBN 0-941410-43-9. $4.95.

*Energy and Equity: Some Social Concerns,* edited by Ellis Cose, 1979. ISBN 0-941410-09-9. $8.50.

*Focus,* JCPS monthly newsletter. ISSN 0740-0195. $12.00 per annum.

*Foreign Trade Policy and Black Economic Advancement: Proceedings of a JCPS Roundtable,* 1981. ISBN 0-941410-19-6. $4.95.

*How to Use Section 5 of the Voting Rights Act,* third edition, Barbara Y. Phillips, 1984. ISBN 0-941410-27-7. $4.95.

*The Impact of the Black Electorate* (Election '84 Report No. 1), Thomas E. Cavanagh, 1984. ISBN 0-941410-44-7. $4.95.

*The JCPS Congressional District Fact Book,* edited by Thomas E. Cavanagh, 1984. ISBN 0-941410-34-X. $5.95.

*Mobilizing the Black Community: The Effects of Personal Contact Campaigning on Black Voters,* Paul Carton, 1984. ISBN 0-941410-45-5.

*National Roster of Black Elected Officials,* volume 12, 1982. ISSN 0092-2935. $23.00.

*The Nineteen Eighties: Prologue and Prospect,* Kenneth B. Clark and John Hope Franklin, 1981. ISBN 0-941410-20-X. $2.95.

*Picking a President: A Guide to Delegate Selection in the States,* JCPS Office of Research, 1980. ISBN 0-941410-15-3. $4.95.

*A Policy Framework for Racial Justice,* (statement by thirty black scholars), 1983. Introduction by Kenneth B. Clark and John Hope Franklin. ISBN 0-941410-30-7. $4.95.

*Public School Desegregation in the United States, 1968-1980,* Gary Orfield, 1983. ISBN 0-941410-29-3. $4.95.

*Race and Political Strategy,* edited by Thomas E. Cavanagh, 1983. ISBN 0-941410-33-1. $4.95.

*Vote Dilution, Minority Voting Rights, and the Courts,* Stephen L. Wasby, 1982. ISBN 0-941410-22-6. $4.95.

*The Voting Rights Act and Black Electoral Participation,* Kenneth H. Thompson, 1982. ISBN 0-941410-24-2. $4.95.

*Wealth and Economic Status: A Perspective on Racial Inequity,* by William P. O'Hare, 1983. ISBN 0-941410-35-8. $4.95.

The Joint Center for Political Studies is a national, nonprofit, tax-exempt institution that conducts research on public policy issues of special concern to black Americans and promotes informed and effective involvement of blacks in the political process. Founded in 1970, the Joint Center provides independent and nonpartisan analyses through research, publication, and outreach programs.

**Joint Center for Political Studies, 1301 Pennsylvania Ave., NW, Washington, DC 20004, 202 626-3500**

**NO LONGER THE PROPERTY OF THE UNIVERSITY OF DELAWARE LIBRARY**

| DATE DUE | | | |
|---|---|---|---|
| DEC 10 1990 | | | |
| | | | |

DEMCO NO. 38-298